The Kingfisher
Picture Number Book

Gill Brackenbury and Jo Hodgkiss

Illustrated by
Sarah Pooley

GUILD PUBLISHING

LONDON · NEW YORK · SYDNEY · TORONTO

Introduction

Here are some of the ways in which you can help children enjoy and learn with this book.

- Let your child explore this book at his or her own pace. Some pages will be flicked over, others will be looked at enthusiastically.

- Encourage your child to explain things in his or her own words. This helps to develop their own understanding of numbers and mathematical concepts.

- Questions throughout the book suggest ways in which to develop number skills but don't just stick to these. Ask other questions and count things on each page.

- Look at the pictures and extend the ideas into your everyday life – when doing the shopping or tidying up, for example. These links with real life are very important for understanding numbers.

- Remember that your children do not have to get the right answer first time. Encourage them to have a go and support their efforts.

Mathematics is an exciting subject. We hope that you and your children will be excited by numbers and have many hours of enjoyment with this book.

Contents

Nought, one, two, three

0

nought

I

one

Nought, one, two, three,
How many bears can you see?

Vicky has filled the train trucks with
bears. Count them and find out if
she has put the right number of
bears in each truck.

2

two

3

three

Four, five, six

four

Four, five, six,
Find the car that's in a fix.

Count the cars.
Has Isabelle put all the cars
into the train trucks?

five

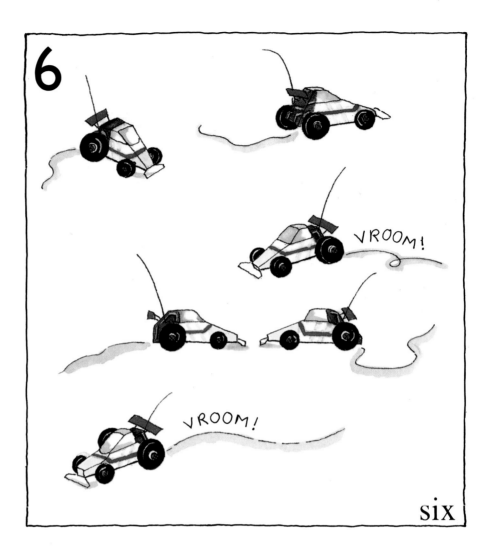

6

VROOM!

VROOM!

six

Seven, eight

7

seven

Seven, eight,
How many dolls are sitting up straight?

Count the dolls in the boxes.
Has Jin Hee put them all
into the train trucks?

8

eight

8   7

13

Nine, ten

nine

Nine, ten,
Robot dogs and robot men.

Count the robots.
How many arms do they have?
Are there the same number of robots
in the trucks?

10

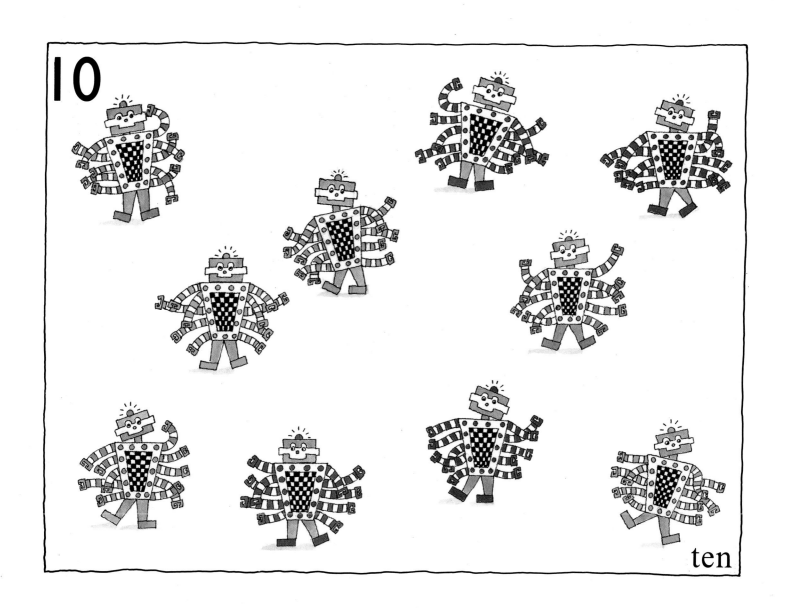

ten

Counting fingers

One finger, two fingers, three fingers . . .
count your fingers up to ten.

All the train trucks are
here but some of the toys
have been taken out.
Can you see where
they are?

Sorting into sets

The children store all the toys in boxes.
Can you sort the toys into the right box?

All the blue things

All the round things

All the big things

All the small things

19

Tidying up

Gertie, Zeff, Anna and Jin Hee are tidying all the dressing-up things into boxes. Can you help them? How many hats go into the hat box?

21

Are there enough?

Is there a hat for everyone?

Are there enough masks for the monsters?

Can you help Zeff, Isabelle, Max and Ben find their shoes? Are there any left over?

The twins need a matching hat, socks and mittens. Can you see them?

Under the sea game

Trapped by an octopus. Count back 2.

A seahorse gives you a ride. Count on 3.

8

9

7

10

11

12

6

Pinched by a crab. Count back 4.

5

4

3

A starfish glows in the dark. Count on 3.

2

You need two or more players to play the game, a counter for each player and a dice.

1

0

Take turns to throw the dice. Move forward for the number shown on the dice. If you land on a red or yellow square, move on or back as the square tells you. The winner is the first one to escape from the shipwreck.

Start here on nought at the bottom of the sea.

24

Building a tower

Dean and Natasha are building a tower. One brick and add on one more brick. That's two bricks.

Two add on one more is three.

26

Three add on one more is four.

Four add on one more is five.

How many bricks?

27

Five fat sausages

If you take one child away from five children, you have four left. Join in the song and take one away.

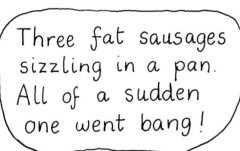

29

Let's go shopping

What would you like to buy at the shops?

31

Corinne's Café

Menu

Cake	2p	Juice	2p
Biscuit	1p	Milk	3p
Roll	3p	Tea	2p
Sandwich	5p	Milkshake	3p
Apple Pie	4p	Lemonade	4p

The prices of food and drink are written on the menu in Corinne's Café.

What can you eat and drink for 10 pence?

The bill for Table One adds up to 18 pence.

How much money did Pauline and Leo spend on Table Two?

33

Cooking

Oscar, Zeff and Katie are making jam tarts. First they measure and weigh the ingredients.

Recipe
Jam Tarts

Ingredients:
125 g butter or margarine
125 g sugar
1 egg
250 g plain flour
pinch of salt
jam

How to make the tarts:

Cream the butter and sugar. Beat the egg and add to the mixture. Stir in the flour and salt. Knead together, then roll out on a floured board. Stamp out shapes using cutters. Place in lightly greased tartlet tins and put a teaspoon of jam in

34

Here they have sorted all the things into sets.

Heavy things   Light things

The pastry cutters are lighter than the spoon.

The packet of flour weighs the same as the packet of sugar.

The jar of jam is heavier than the eggs.

The tea party

Share the tarts so that Pauline and Zeff have the same number each.

 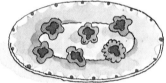

Now share twelve onto three plates.

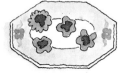  

Then share twelve
onto four plates.

And share twelve
onto six plates.

What size are your feet?

Gertie needs a new pair of shoes. She is size ten.

Measure your foot here and find out your shoe size.

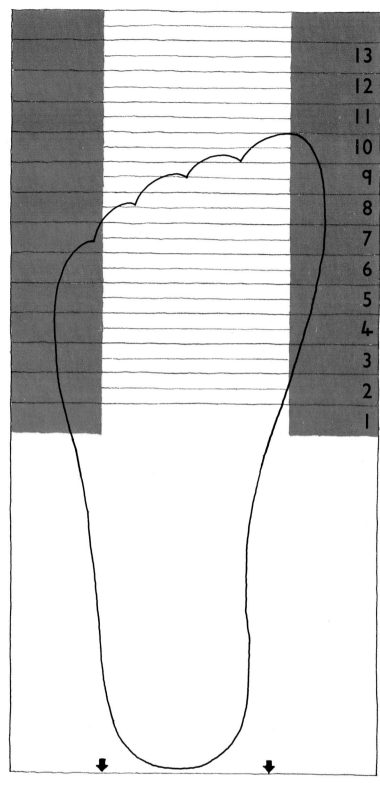

I'm size nine.

Your feet must have grown. Now they. are size ten.

Too big   Too small   Too big   Too small

These shoes are just the right size.

The boots and shoes fit inside these boxes but which ones?

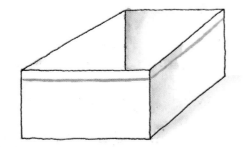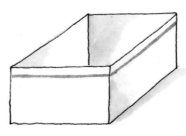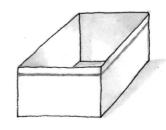

39

Measuring

All the children are measuring things today.

tall

taller

tallest

I'm the tallest! I'm the Giant!

I'm measuring with my hands.

I'm a big bunny!

short   shorter   shortest

Which snake is the longest?

long   longer   longest

The hospital

Jin Hee's teddy is ill. This is what he does to look after him at different times of the day.

calendar

MAY				
Sat		6	13	20	27
Sun		7	14	21	28
Mon	1	8	15	22	29
Tue	2	9	16	23	30
Wed	3	10	17	24	31
Thur	4	11	18	25	
Fri	5	12	19	26	

Seven o'clock   **07.00**

Time to wake up.

Half past nine   **09.30**

Time to take your temperature.

Eleven o'clock   **11.00**

Time for medicine.

Half past twelve   **12.30**

Time for lunch.

A calendar tells us the days of the week and the date in the year. Clocks and watches tell us the time.

Clocks

Two o'clock   **14.00**

Time to see the doctor.

Four o'clock   **16.00**

Time for a story.

Half past five   **17.30**

Time for supper.

Seven o'clock   **19.00**

Time for bed.

Birthdays

Alice is just four days old. Look how many
presents she has.
Vicky and Zeff and their friends are making
a graph to show how old they are.
How many candles would you have?

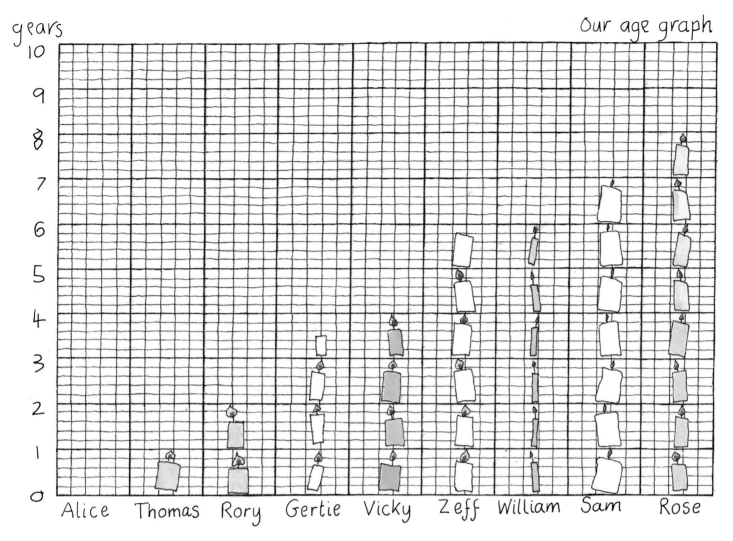

45